THE JPS B'NAI MITZVAH TORAH COMMENTARY

Be-har (Leviticus 25:1–26:2)
Haftarah (Jeremiah 32:6–27)

Rabbi Jeffrey K. Salkin

The Jewish Publication Society · Philadelphia
University of Nebraska Press · Lincoln

INTRODUCTION

News flash: the most important thing about becoming bar or bat mitzvah isn't the party. Nor is it the presents. Nor even being able to celebrate with your family and friends—as wonderful as those things are. Nor is it even standing before the congregation and reading the prayers of the liturgy—as important as that is.

No, the most important thing about becoming bar or bat mitzvah is sharing Torah with the congregation. And why is that? Because of all Jewish skills, that is the most important one.

Here is what is true about rites of passage: you can tell what a culture values by the tasks it asks its young people to perform on their way to maturity. In American culture, you become responsible for driving, responsible for voting, and yes, responsible for drinking responsibly.

In some cultures, the rite of passage toward maturity includes some kind of trial, or a test of strength. Sometimes, it is a kind of "outward bound" camping adventure. Among the Maasai tribe in Africa, it is traditional for a young person to hunt and kill a lion. In some Hispanic cultures, fifteen year-old girls celebrate the *quinceañera*, which marks their entrance into maturity.

What is Judaism's way of marking maturity? It combines both of these rites of passage: *responsibility* and *test*. You show that you are on your way to becoming a *responsible* Jewish adult through a public *test* of strength and knowledge—reading or chanting Torah, and then teaching it to the congregation.

This is the most important Jewish ritual mitzvah (commandment), and that is how you demonstrate that you are, truly, bar or bat mitzvah—old enough to be responsible for the mitzvot.

What Is Torah?

So, what exactly is the Torah? You probably know this already, but let's review.

The Torah (teaching) consists of "the five books of Moses," sometimes also called the *chumash* (from the Hebrew word *chameish,* which means "five"), or, sometimes, the Greek word Pentateuch (which means "the five teachings").

Here are the five books of the Torah, with their common names and their Hebrew names.

> **Genesis (The beginning), which in Hebrew is Bere'shit (from the first words—"When God began to create").** Bere'shit spans the years from Creation to Joseph's death in Egypt. Many of the Bible's best stories are in Genesis: the creation story itself; Adam and Eve in the Garden of Eden; Cain and Abel; Noah and the Flood; and the tales of the Patriarchs and Matriarchs, Abraham, Isaac, Jacob, Sarah, Rebekah, Rachel, and Leah. It also includes one of the greatest pieces of world literature, the story of Joseph, which is actually the oldest complete novel in history, comprising more than one-quarter of all Genesis.

> **Exodus (Getting out), which in Hebrew is Shemot (These are the names).** Exodus begins with the story of the Israelite slavery in Egypt. It then moves to the rise of Moses as a leader, and the Israelites' liberation from slavery. After the Israelites leave Egypt, they experience the miracle of the parting of the Sea of Reeds (or "Red Sea"); the giving of the Ten Commandments at Mount Sinai; the idolatry of the Golden Calf; and the design and construction of the Tabernacle and of the ark for the original tablets of the law, which our ancestors carried with them in the desert. Exodus also includes various ethical and civil laws, such as "You shall not wrong a stranger or oppress him, for you were strangers in the land of Egypt" (22:20).

> **Leviticus (about the Levites), or, in Hebrew, Va-yikra' (And God called).** It goes into great detail about the kinds of sacrifices that the ancient Israelites brought as offerings; the laws of ritual purity; the animals that were permitted and forbidden for eating (the beginnings of the tradition of kashrut, the Jewish dietary laws); the diagnosis of various skin diseases; the ethical laws of holiness; the ritual calendar of the Jewish year; and various agricultural laws concerning the treatment of the Land of Israel. Leviticus is basically the manual of ancient Judaism.

> Numbers (because the book begins with the census of the Israelites), or, in Hebrew, Be-midbar (In the wilderness). The book describes the forty years of wandering in the wilderness and the various rebellions against Moses. The constant theme: "Egypt wasn't so bad. Maybe we should go back." The greatest rebellion against Moses was the negative reports of the spies about the Land of Israel, which discouraged the Israelites from wanting to move forward into the land. For that reason, the "wilderness generation" must die off before a new generation can come into maturity and finish the journey.

> Deuteronomy (The repetition of the laws of the Torah), or, in Hebrew, Devarim (The words). The final book of the Torah is, essentially, Moses's farewell address to the Israelites as they prepare to enter the Land of Israel. Here we find various laws that had been previously taught, though sometimes with different wording. Much of Deuteronomy contains laws that will be important to the Israelites as they enter the Land of Israel—laws concerning the establishment of a monarchy and the ethics of warfare. Perhaps the most famous passage from Deuteronomy contains the *Shema*, the declaration of God's unity and uniqueness, and the *Ve-ahavta*, which follows it. Deuteronomy ends with the death of Moses on Mount Nebo as he looks across the Jordan Valley into the land that he will not enter.

Jews read the Torah in sequence—starting with Bere'shit right after Simchat Torah in the autumn, and then finishing Devarim on the following Simchat Torah. Each Torah portion is called a parashah (division; sometimes called a *sidrah,* a place in the order of the Torah reading). The stories go around in a full circle, reminding us that we can always gain more insights and more wisdom from the Torah. This means that if you don't "get" the meaning this year, don't worry—it will come around again.

And What Else? The Haftarah

We read or chant the Torah from the Torah scroll—the most sacred thing that a Jewish community has in its possession. The Torah is written without vowels, and the ability to read it and chant it is part of the challenge and the test.

But there is more to the synagogue reading. Every Torah reading has an accompanying haftarah reading. Haftarah means "conclusion," because there was once a time when the service actually ended with that reading. Some scholars believe that the reading of the haftarah originated at a time when non-Jewish authorities outlawed the reading of the Torah, and the Jews read the haftarah sections instead. In fact, in some synagogues, young people who become bar or bat mitzvah read very little Torah and instead read the entire haftarah portion.

The haftarah portion comes from the Nevi'im, the prophetic books, which are the second part of the Jewish Bible. It is either read or chanted from a Hebrew Bible, or maybe from a booklet or a photocopy.

The ancient sages chose the haftarah passages because their themes reminded them of the words or stories in the Torah text. Sometimes, they chose *haftarah* with special themes in honor of a festival or an upcoming festival.

Not all books in the prophetic section of the Hebrew Bible consist of prophecy. Several are historical. For example:

The book of Joshua tells the story of the conquest and settlement of Israel.

The book of Judges speaks of the period of early tribal rulers who would rise to power, usually for the purpose of uniting the tribes in war against their enemies. Some of these leaders are famous: Deborah, the great prophetess and military leader, and Samson, the biblical strong man.

The books of Samuel start with Samuel, the last judge, and then move to the creation of the Israelite monarchy under Saul and David (approximately 1000 BCE).

The books of Kings tell of the death of King David, the rise of King Solomon, and how the Israelite kingdom split into the Northern Kingdom of Israel and the Southern Kingdom of Judah (approximately 900 BCE).

And then there are the books of the prophets, those spokesmen for God whose words fired the Jewish conscience. Their names are immortal: Isaiah, Jeremiah, Ezekiel, Amos, Hosea, among others.

Someone once said: "There is no evidence of a biblical prophet ever being invited back a second time for dinner." Why? Because the prophets were tough. They had no patience for injustice, apathy, or hypocrisy. No one escaped their criticisms. Here's what they taught:

> God commands the Jews to behave decently toward one another. In fact, God cares more about basic ethics and decency than about ritual behavior.
> God chose the Jews *not* for special privileges, but for special duties to humanity.
> As bad as the Jews sometimes were, there was always the possibility that they would improve their behavior.
> As bad as things might be now, it will not always be that way. Someday, there will be universal justice and peace. Human history is moving forward toward an ultimate conclusion that some call the Messianic Age: a time of universal peace and prosperity for the Jewish people and for all the people of the world.

Your Mission—To Teach Torah to the Congregation

On the day when you become bar or bat mitzvah, you will be reading, or chanting, Torah—in Hebrew. You will be reading, or chanting, the haftarah—in Hebrew. That is the major skill that publicly marks the becoming of bar or bat mitzvah. But, perhaps even more important than that, you need to be able to teach something about the Torah portion, and perhaps the haftarah as well.

And that is where this book comes in. It will be a very valuable resource for you, and your family, in the b'nai mitzvah process. Here is what you will find in it:

> A brief **summary** of every Torah portion. This is a basic overview of the portion; and, while it might not refer to everything in the Torah portion, it will explain its most important aspects.
> A list of the **major ideas** in the Torah portion. The purpose: to make the Torah portion real, in ways that we can relate to. Every Torah portion contains unique ideas, and when you put all

of those ideas together, you actually come up with a list of Judaism's most important ideas.

› Two *divrei Torah* ("words of Torah," or "sermonettes") for each portion. These *divrei Torah* explain significant aspects of the Torah portion in accessible, reader-friendly language. Each *devar Torah* contains references to **traditional** Jewish sources (those that were written before the modern era), as well as **modern** sources and quotes. We have searched, far and wide, to find sources that are unusual, interesting, and not just the "same old stuff" that many people already know about the Torah portion. Why did we include these minisermons in the volume? Not because we want you to simply copy those sermons and pass them off as your own (that would be cheating), though you are free to quote from them. We included them so that you can see what is possible—how you can try to make meaning for yourself out of the words of Torah.

› **Connections:** This is perhaps the most valuable part. It's a list of questions that you can ask yourself, or that others might help you think about—any of which can lead to the creation of your *devar Torah.*

Note: you don't have to like everything that's in a particular Torah portion. Some aren't that loveable. Some are hard to understand; some are about religious practices that people today might find confusing, and even offensive; some contain ideas that we might find totally outmoded.

But this doesn't have to get in the way. After all, most kids spend a lot of time thinking about stories that contain ideas that modern people would find totally bizarre. Any good medieval fantasy story falls into that category.

And we also believe that, if you spend just a little bit of time with those texts, you can begin to understand what the author was trying to say.

This volume goes one step further. Sometimes, the haftarah comes off as a second thought, and no one really thinks about it. We have tried to solve that problem by including a **summary** of each haftarah, and then a mini-sermon on the haftarah. This will help you learn how these sacred words are relevant to today's world, and even to your own life.

All Bible quotations come from the NJPS translation, which is found in the many different editions of the JPS TANAKH; in the Conservative movement's *Etz Hayim: Torah and Commentary;* in the Reform movement's *Torah: A Modern Commentary;* and in other Bible commentaries and study guides.

How Do I Write a *Devar Torah?*

It really is easier than it looks.

There are many ways of thinking about the *devar Torah.* It is, of course, a short sermon on the meaning of the Torah (and, perhaps, the haftarah) portion. It might even be helpful to think of the *devar Torah* as a "book report" on the portion itself.

The most important thing you can know about this sacred task is: *Learn* the words. *Love* the words. Teach people what it could mean to *live* the words.

Here's a basic outline for a *devar Torah:*

"My Torah portion is (name of portion) _____,
   from the book of _____, chapter
   _____.

"In my Torah portion, we learn that_____
   (Summary of portion)

"For me, the most important lesson of this Torah portion is (what is the best thing in the portion? Take the portion as a whole; your *devar Torah* does not have to be only, or specifically, on the verses that you are reading).

"As I learned my Torah portion, I found myself wondering:
   ➤ *Raise a question that the Torah portion itself raises.*
   ➤ *"Pick a fight"* with the portion. Argue with it.
   ➤ *Answer a question* that is listed in the "Connections" section of each Torah portion.
   ➤ *Suggest a question to your rabbi* that you would want the rabbi to answer in his or her own *devar Torah* or sermon.

"I have lived the values of the Torah by _____
(here, you can talk about how the Torah portion relates to your
own life. If you have done a mitzvah project, you can talk about
that here).

How To Keep It from Being Boring
(and You from Being Bored)

Some people just don't like giving traditional speeches. From our per-
spective, that's really okay. Perhaps you can teach Torah in a different
way—one that makes sense to you.

> ➤ Write an "open letter" to one of the characters in your Torah por-
> tion. "Dear Abraham: I hope that your trip to Canaan was not too
> hard . . ." "Dear Moses: Were you afraid when you got the Ten
> Commandments on Mount Sinai? I sure would have been . . ."
> ➤ Write a news story about what happens. Imagine yourself to
> be a television or news reporter. "Residents of neighboring cit-
> ies were horrified yesterday as the wicked cities of Sodom and
> Gomorrah were burned to the ground. Some say that God was
> responsible . . ."
> ➤ Write an imaginary interview with a character in your Torah portion.
> ➤ Tell the story from the point of view of another character, or a mi-
> nor character, in the story. For instance, tell the story of the Gar-
> den of Eden from the point of view of the serpent. Or the story
> of the Binding of Isaac from the point of view of the ram, which
> was substituted for Isaac as a sacrifice. Or perhaps the story of
> the sale of Joseph from the point of view of his coat, which was
> stripped off him and dipped in a goat's blood.
> ➤ Write a poem about your Torah portion.
> ➤ Write a song about your Torah portion.
> ➤ Write a play about your Torah portion, and have some friends act
> it out with you.
> ➤ Create a piece of artwork about your Torah portion.

The bottom line is: Make this a joyful experience. Yes—it could
even be fun.

The Very Last Thing You Need to Know at This Point

The Torah scroll is written without vowels. Why? Don't *sofrim* (Torah scribes) know the vowels?

Of course they do.

So, why do they leave the vowels out?

One reason is that the Torah came into existence at a time when sages were still arguing about the proper vowels, and the proper pronunciation.

But here is another reason: The Torah text, as we have it today, and as it sits in the scroll, is actually *an unfinished work*. Think of it: the words are just sitting there. Because they have no vowels, it is as if they have no voice.

When we read the Torah publicly, we give voice to the ancient words. And when we find meaning in those ancient words, and we talk about those meanings, those words jump to life. They enter our lives. They make our world deeper and better.

Mazal tov to you, and your family. This is your journey toward Jewish maturity. Love it.

THE TORAH

❖ Be-har: Leviticus 25:1–26:2

The book of Leviticus has been a wild ride: from details about sacrifices, to laws about animals that you can and cannot eat; to skin diseases and other bodily issues; to laws about priests and the sacred days of the ancient Jewish calendar . . . and, now, to the way that Jews must treat the Land of Israel. Just as the Israelites must observe the Sabbath, the land itself needs a Sabbath—"resting" after six years of sowing and pruning. Then, every fifty years, the land has to return to its original owners, who might have lost their land due to financial difficulty.

Leviticus began with an exhausting description of offerings to God, offerings that actually came from God and belong to God. It turns out that the Land of Israel itself is like a sacred offering, which also belongs to God.

Summary

- Every seven years the Land of Israel must observe a Sabbath. Like people, the land must be allowed to "rest." This is known as the *shemitah,* or sabbatical, year. (25:1–7)
- Every fifty years people who had lost their land due to economic disaster are allowed to reclaim their property. The Hebrew term for this is *dror* (release from economic servitude) and the fiftieth year is known as the *yovel* year. It is proclaimed on Yom Kippur, and it begins with the blast of the shofar.
- If someone is in economic trouble and has to sell part of his or her property, that person's nearest relative must redeem what his relative has sold. (25:25–28)
- If your kinsman becomes poor, do not loan money to him or her on interest, or treat him or her as a slave. (25:35–46)

The Big Ideas

> **The Land of Israel—indeed, the entire earth—belongs to God.** Human beings are only the stewards, or managers, of the land. It is therefore human responsibility to take care of God's gift to human beings, and to make sure that it is not abused and that it is allowed to replenish itself. In that sense, the land is like a human being—it, too, needs a Sabbath.

> **Owning is temporary.** This may be the most radical text in the entire Torah. Imagine: if a family becomes impoverished and has to sell its land, it can reclaim that land after the fiftieth year. This is so important that it is actually written on the Liberty Bell: "Proclaim liberty throughout the land unto all the inhabitants thereof" (25:10). But "liberty" doesn't only mean freedom from political oppression; it means freedom from eternal economic oppression. That is what the Torah wants to abolish—the idea that people would always be poor.

> ***Tzedakah* begins with those who are closest to us.** Many people care passionately about poor people who live on the other side of the world, and people they will never meet. While this is noble, it is far nobler to pay attention to those who are closest to you— your immediate relatives.

> **Family is family.** Yes, our moral responsibilities begin with those who are closest to us—our relatives. And yet, sometimes we have to fight the temptation to be cruel to them, and to take advantage of their weaknesses, maybe even their impoverished state. That is why the laws about taking care of your relatives end with the proclamation: "I the Lord am your God, who brought you of the land of Egypt" (25:38). Don't become a Pharaoh to your family!

Divrei Torah
JEWISH MATH CLASS

Quick, math whizzes: what "base" is our mathematical system based on? Right: base ten.

Okay, now for the Jewish math class: what numerical "base" is Judaism based on?

Answer: Seven.

It turns out that all of Judaism is based on the number seven. Here goes: The seventh day of the week is holy—Shabbat. And the seventh month of the year is especially holy—Tishrei, which is when Rosh Hashanah, Yom Kippur, and Sukkot occur. (That's if you start counting the year with the first month, Nisan. But what if you start counting the year with Tishrei? Then the seventh month becomes Nisan—which is when Pesach occurs. Also deeply holy.) We can call either of these seventh months the "expanded Shabbat." As Rabbi Saul Berman notes: "God's creation of the universe in seven periods of time is celebrated not only on the seventh day, but on the seventh of every natural time period."

Okay, a Shabbat of days, and a Shabbat of months. And in this Torah portion, we meet a Shabbat of years. Every seventh year, the land lies fallow—the *shemitah* year. (By the way, sometimes teachers and spiritual leaders get their own *shemitah* year. It's called a sabbatical—from the word "Sabbath.") It's not only that the land lies fallow; there's something else that happens, or doesn't happen. Deut. 15:2 adds something to the *shemitah* observance: during this time you can't collect debts from those who owe you money!

Oh, wait—there's more. Multiply seven times seven (which gets you forty-nine), and then add one—which gets you fifty. Every fifty years, property must return to its original inhabitants, who might have lost it because of economic hardship. That's the *yovel*—which we sometimes translate as "jubilee." Was it ever really observed? Probably not. But that didn't stop American blacks from declaring that the year of Lincoln's Emancipation Proclamation (1863) was, in fact, a jubilee year.

The Torah portion begins by telling us that these laws were given on Mount Sinai, a big deal. But why? you might ask. That's exactly what some ancient sages asked: "'The Lord spoke to Moses on Mount Sinai': Why is *shemitah* connected with Mount Sinai? Weren't all the commandments said from Sinai?"

Why is this big? Because the Exodus from Egypt was not just a bunch of Hebrew slaves escaping from Pharaoh. It was intended to create a social revolution. It's as if God were saying to the Israelites: First, I am going to bring you into the Land of Israel. This is my gift to you. Be good to it. Don't abuse it. And not only that. Every seventh year you have to cancel debts! And every fifty years, all economic injustices are healed! People are not meant to be physically or economically oppressed forever.

True freedom means equality and responsibility. Every once in a while society needs a reset. A radical notion and a lofty goal, then— and now.

WHOSE POOR COME FIRST?

The imaginary synagogue Congregation Or Tzedek (Light of justice) requires that all candidates complete a mitzvah project as part of their preparation for becoming bar or bat mitzvah. This is pretty much standard operating procedure for many synagogues. The purpose is to teach kids that acts of giving are an essential part of Jewish life. The old joke is that it's not just about the "bar" it's also about the "mitzvah."

Three kids from our imaginary synagogue are having a discussion about their projects.

Ivan: "I'm giving a portion of my bar mitzvah gift money to our local Jewish Federation. After all, they help elderly Jews in our community. Plus, they give money to Jewish kids to go to summer camp. I feel like I owe them."

Jennifer: "That is so narrow-minded! I am donating a portion of my bat mitzvah money to our local symphony. After all, all kinds of people love music."

Alex: "I'm giving a portion to the needy in Africa. After all, they need it the most."

Conversations like these actually happen—a lot. Some Jews are *universalists*—"we should take care of everyone." And some are *particularists*—"we should take of ourselves." Some people think that

Jews should be saving the rain forests, or helping animals. And others believe that Jews should only give to specifically Jewish causes.

And it all gets a little bit more complicated because the "non-Jewish" causes that some Jews support—environment, helping animals, curing illnesses—are all connected to Jewish values. Judaism talks about both *tikkun olam* (healing the world) and *k'lal Yisrael* (caring for your own).

Let's go back to the Torah portion. It clearly says that if your relatives become poor you are to take care of them. This becomes a core Jewish principle. According to the Shulhan Arukh, the most important compilation of Jewish law: "The poor of your city take precedence over the poor of another city. The needy of Israel receive priority over the poor of the Diaspora. Obligations to local resident poor precede those owed to transient poor who have just come into the city. One's impoverished family members come before another poor person."

Judaism teaches that you best learn how to take care of other people, and the wider world, when you "practice" on your own people. While the expression "charity begins at home" is not a Jewish one, it might be; however, Judaism would add, "so long as it doesn't end at home."

Israeli Prime Minister Menachem Begin cared passionately about his own people but sometimes it seemed that he was disinterested in the rest of the world. Yet Rabbi Daniel Gordis writes: "In 1977, when desperate Vietnamese boat people were plucked from the high seas by an Israeli freighter, after ships from other countries had ignored them, Begin, in what was essentially his first act as prime minister, ordered that they be brought to Israel, where he made them citizens."

Yes, we should care about our fellow Jews first. And when we get good at it, we should care about others too.

Connections

> What do you think of the idea of letting the land lie fallow (*shemitah*)?

> How about returning land to its original owners (*yovel*)?

> What could be some problems associated with these concepts?

> Why do you think that the *yovel* was never put into practice?

> If the *yovel*, or jubilee year, probably never really happened, why continue to learn about it?

> Do you agree that supporting one's own poor takes precedence over supporting other people? What could be some of the problems in doing so?

THE HAFTARAH

❖ Be-har: Jeremiah 32:6–27

Think of any impoverished, desolate, crime-ridden area of a major city. Go there with your parents. Suggest to them: "Hey, we should buy some property here!" Chances are they will tell you that you're crazy.

Now, take your parents and travel to a war zone. Everything has been destroyed. Suggest to your parents: "Hey, let's buy some property here!" If, in fact, they have even agreed to make the trip in the first place, they will tell you to get back in the taxi because we're going home as quickly as we can.

That is precisely the situation that Jeremiah is facing. The Babylonian army has destroyed the city of Jerusalem, and, right then, Jeremiah's cousin Hanamel asks the prophet to help him out. He lost his land due to economic reverses, a situation similar to what this week's Torah portion describes. The Torah makes it clear: relatives have to step in, buy back the land, and put the person back on his feet. That is exactly what Hanamel asks Jeremiah to do—to redeem his portion of land in the Jerusalem suburb of Anathoth.

And Jeremiah does it. To be a prophet is to testify to the power of hope, and that the future will be better than the present. Jeremiah's faith in the land and its future can inspire everyone.

Why Jews Care about Israel

Why do Jews care so much about a piece of land called Israel, and the people who live there?

It should be pretty easy to figure out the answer to that question, shouldn't it? After all, the Land of Israel was the place where the ancestors of the Jewish people lived—ever since the time of Abraham. Even though they were exiled from the land several times (the Assyrians destroyed the Northern Kingdom of Israel; the Babylonians destroyed the Southern Kingdom of Judah; and, centuries later, the Romans exiled the Jews from the land), the Jews never stopped dreaming about the Land of Israel.

When Jews pray, they face Jerusalem. Jewish prayers contain hopes that the Land of Israel will be restored to them—and that God will come back to Zion as well. As it is written in the prayer book, "May our eyes behold Your compassionate return to Zion. Blessed is Adonai, who restores the Divine Presence to Zion."

Jews know that they can move to Israel if they need to, if anti-Semitism becomes intolerable in the countries where they live. Jews take pride in Israel's achievements—in areas such as medical research, science, technology, culture, and education. Jews take pride in Israel's military accomplishments, in its ability to stand up to hostile neighbors. That pride in Israel is powerful, even when Jews disagree over the precise details of how Israel should handle the many societal, political, and military challenges that it faces.

All of that is important, but there is something else about Israel that is central to the way Jews view themselves: Israel embodies their hope in the future.

That's what Jeremiah is talking about. And he put his money where his mouth is. Even as Jerusalem was about to be destroyed, Jeremiah knew that he had the responsibility to redeem his family's land in order to fulfill the Torah portion's commandments of land redemption. It must have seemed crazy, but Jeremiah had a sense that his land purchase was part of Jewish history, for he laid out the entire history of the Jews—going back to the Exodus from Egypt (32:20–22). Jeremiah believed that buying back the land was part of the Jewish history of hope. He knew his act was a symbolic one, so he made sure to publicize it with the help of his media consultant (scribe) Baruch.

And so it is that when Jews get married one of the prayers is this: "Yet again it shall be heard, in the cities of Judah and in the streets of Jerusalem—the sound of joy and gladness, the voice of bride and groom." A wedding is a moment of hope, and the wedding couple brings the ultimate hope—the hope for return to the Land of Israel—into that moment of love.

Jeremiah's example lives for us today. As Rabbi Yitz Greenberg writes: "Today, Jews are back in Israel and facing the prospect of peace and prosperity in the land. This miraculous achievement was made possible by loyalty and love even under fire, by buying and building even in the face of defeat, through hope and trust in God even when it appeared to be hopeless. Thus Jewish history proves that life, love and hope are stronger than death, selfishness and despair."

No wonder that, at the end of the Passover seder, we sing "Next year in Jerusalem!" and that the Israeli national anthem is called "Hatikvah"—The Hope.

❖ Notes

CPSIA information can be obtained
at www.ICGtesting.com
Printed in the USA
LVHW091625011218
598911LV00001B/63/P